ISBN 978-1-331-36686-7
PIBN 10180131

1 MONTH OF
FREE
READING

at
www.ForgottenBooks.com

By purchasing this book you are
eligible for one month membership to
ForgottenBooks.com, giving you
unlimited access to our entire
collection of over 700,000 titles via
our web site and mobile apps.

To claim your free month visit:

www.forgottenbooks.com/free180131

English
Français
Deutsche
Italiano
Español
Português

www.forgottenbooks.com

Mythology Photography **Fiction**
Fishing Christianity **Art** Cooking
Essays Buddhism Freemasonry
Medicine **Biology** Music **Ancient
Egypt** Evolution Carpentry Physics
Dance Geology **Mathematics** Fitness
Shakespeare **Folklore** Yoga Marketing
Confidence Immortality Biographies
Poetry **Psychology** Witchcraft
Electronics Chemistry History **Law**
Accounting **Philosophy** Anthropology
Alchemy Drama Quantum Mechanics
Atheism Sexual Health **Ancient History**
Entrepreneurship Languages Sport
Paleontology Needlework Islam
Metaphysics Investment Archaeology
Parenting Statistics Criminology
Motivational

TEXTILE EDUCATION AMONG THE PURITANS.

BY

C. J. H. WOODBURY, Sc. D.

Read before

The Bostonian Society,

COUNCIL CHAMBER, OLD STATE HOUSE,

BOSTON, MASS.

April 18th, 1911.

TEXTILE EDUCATION AMONG THE PURITANS.

BY

C. J. H. WOODBURY, Sc. D.

Read before

The Bostonian Society,

COUNCIL CHAMBER, OLD STATE HOUSE,

BOSTON, MASS.

April 18th, 1911

TS
WG

TEXTILE EDUCATION AMONG THE PURITANS.

The more spectacular religious and governmental oppressions of that day often overshadow the economic conditions which were fundamental elements in the settlement of New England by the English.

England had been growing poorer in common with continental Europe. Population had gradually grown, and the primitive conditions of husbandry failed to increase crops commensurate with the greater consumption, and handiwork had not received the aid of machinery to develop the larger production of cloth.

None are too poor to fight and the burden of wars, both civil and foreign, throughout Europe perhaps developed irritation and discontent of poverty which made taxation by the state and rates of the church especially onerous burdens. The whole story of daily existence in Europe was told by the Pilgrim author in three words, " Life was hard."

The details of war, rather that the greater victories of peace, usurp the pages of history, and in like manner the printed books of colonial days are largely devoted to polemics among the clergy, relations with the Indians, and a great amount of petty legislation inevitable with the conditions of a new country, while the events of daily life which led to substantial results in the founding of a nation were rarely printed, and such as exist were, for the most part, found in old letters, inventories and accounts.

Outside of the daily press, a comparable condition as to the record of commercial affairs, exists with us today.

Of the many in England discontented with their lot, there

were some who had available resources sufficient to come to Massachusetts Bay, which had been visited for many years and mapped for over twenty years.

Whatever may have been the desires of many to emigrate, travelling to colonize was an expensive matter, available only to the prosperous.

The selective character of the New England colonists was as well understood as it is today, and in a sermon WILLIAM STOUGHTON said, "God sifted a whole nation that he might send choice Grain over into this Wilderness."

The Puritan pioneers were not poverty stricken refugees, and their sufferings were largely due to ignorance of more severe climatic conditions than those of the old country, which they were not prepared to meet, and it was merely a lack of available resources at the first.

It is strictly in line with what is to be presented in this paper on their fertile expedients to provide themselves with cloth that a reference should be made to their domestic ingenuity such as their origin of banking around houses, placing clay between the studding and keeping it in place with clay-boards, now known as clap-boards, anticipating building-paper, by birch bark under shingles which has been known to last over a century, and packing houses with seaweed to keep out all land vermin,— later the subject material of a patent not yet expired. In their meeting houses was originated the closed pew, in place of open benches of the old country with their inevitable drafts. The origin of foot-stoves has eluded all my searches for an answer, but I cannot learn that they were ever known in England, although the later introduction of large stoves into meeting houses divided at least one parish at the time of the Arminian schism.

Whenever a glimpse of their daily life can be obtained, there is found most fertile resourcefulness of method.

It has been estimated that the fifteen hundred who came to Salem in 1628-30 brought with them property to the amount of fully a million dollars. Silks, furs, and plate abounded in the colony and yet in a few years there was such a shortage of cloth that sheep skin garments became a necessity.

The dress of the period for both men and women in circumstances to have their portraits painted, which appears to be the best measure of prosperity and social standing in early days, was elaborate in cut, color, and decoration, and the right to the dress of the gentleman or the gentlewoman was fixed by statute in Massachusetts Bay, as it was in England, limiting the privileges of wearing gold and silver lace and other ornaments to those of estates above certain amounts.

Inventories and also correspondence with the old country, ordering outfits, contain a vast amount of dandified detail.

Wherever there were instances of unusual prosperity, conditions akin to an aristocracy prevailed. The prosperous class were Tories almost to a man as they or their wives did not wish the supply of luxuries of dress from abroad stopped. The Revolution by the impoverishment or the expatriation of these Tories brought these aristocratic assumptions to an end.

Later simplicity leading to fashions of the present day in men's garb, at least, may have been forced by the scarcity of varied fabrics and more especially the material for ornamentation.

Although I shall run from the Colony to the Province, as the facts may lead, the purpose of this paper is to call attention to the fertility of mental resources exercised by this seashore colony in providing themselves with cloth when a sufficient supply could not be obtained from the mother country, and vexatious as her commercial prohibitions may have appeared, it is evident that the earlier laws of this nature were defensive, because England had not the wool to spare. The Pilgrim writer claimed that " warrs had kept down the sheepe."

Two irrelevent conditions proved to be of vital benefit to the Colony, first: the efforts of Elizabeth to reform the methods of taxation, by equalization as people had means to pay without undue distress and not to rest directly upon agriculture, had not been fully developed under Charles the first, and indeed contains open questions to this day; but she performed one act ultimately of untold value to the colonists of Massachusetts Bay, who came from the eastern counties of England in the very territory where she had colonized spinners and weavers from the Netherlands and these people had taught others of their skill, so that these Puritan emigrants were the best equipped of all England to spin and weave.

The general exercise of such skill undoubtedly became a necessity rather than an early intention among the Colonists.

Another condition helpful to the Colony was the fact that the increasing scarcity of meat had impelled those living in the shore countries of England and Europe to go after fish, and finding the great supply of cod in the north Atlantic they sailed the high seas and developed a race of skilled navigators from Scandanavia to the Mediterranean, who traversed the ocean to great distances in small boats whose return to port was evidence of bold seamanship.

While Endicott's Colony did not contain many fishermen, those of the Dorchester Colony which came from Devonshire, which reaches from the English Channel to the Bristol Channel, who earlier came to Cape Ann and thence to Salem, and the Manxmen who later came to Marblehead,— and brought their dialect with them,— were fishermen, who added to the strength of the little Colony whose fortunes they shared.

THE PURITAN PURPOSE.

While the charter of the Massachusetts Bay Colony recites its purpose to be the conversion of the Indians to the Christian religion, yet it is an historical fact that the Puritans came over for business rather than for sentiment, and when a Marble-header interrupted the minister with "we came here to fish, and not to worship God," he undoutedly vied with the sermon in an irreverent declaration of truth, with out any disparagement to the "soundness" of the longer discourse from the pulpit.

They intended to catch fish for the English market, but in fact, were forced to send them to the West Indies and Spain in order to obtain cotton and wool.   They expected to buy beaver skins from the Indians on their own terms, but the savages were such keen traders that the struggle for self-preservation developed the proverbial Yankee shrewdness.

They expected to depend upon the old country for supplies, even to their drink, for there was such a general belief in England that the water in America was unfit for drink, owing doubtless to the brackishness of tide-washed springs at the shore where early travelers filled their water butts, that Endicott's fleet was ballasted with casks of ale.

Even angle worms were brought over for bait in fresh water fishing and the English angle worm, a different species from those indigenous to this country, still exists in some localities.

It may be difficult to state their economic intentions other than to remain a loyal, subservient colony, but the neglect of the Mother Country followed by repressive commercial legislation developed their mental resources into an independent condition, a century before it was one of record.

No one with facts at hand can pretend that this was a land of liberty, for there was greater personal freedom in England as the very fact of the thousands of non-conformists who remained there, either in relative peace or to fight out their differences, attests.

This colony was no democracy, Governor JOHN WINTHROP, the broadest mind among them, inveigled most bitterly against general representation.   The first freemen were qualified May 18, 1631, and a count of those so elevated above their fellow-men up to 1641 when the population was first known, showed that out of a colony of 21,000, there had been 1,293 qualified as freemen although on account of death and returns to England, the maximum number at any one time was probably less than 1,000 freemen.

In a country fringing the seacoast, although their charter conferred jurisdiction westerly to the " South Sea," yet they were content with the judgment of an exploring party sent out from Salem who reported that the country was not worth the while of more than one plantation running back a league from the sea, save at some places where two leagues might be worth the while.

These pioneers were of that middle English stock still feeling the pride of strength from the advancement which they had received at the expense of the prestige of the aristocracy as some of the results of the wars of the Roses which rehabilitated England, except as to the condition of the peasant farm laborers which continued as before.

The extent to which this little band fringed between the savages and the deep sea developed their own self reliance is shown by the manner in which they applied the principles of law, developed under generations of monarchies, to the solution of problems of local self government, and beyond that they initiated new functions of government, notably the written ballot, trade schools, industrial statistics, free public education, the town government, the separation of church and state, citizen militia, printed paper money and the record of deeds and mortgages. Well did Carlyle characterize the people who showed such an initiative as " the last of the heroisms."

COTTON AT THE TIME OF THE COLONY.

The relation of England and the North American colonies to cotton contain some unexpected anomalies.

Cotton appears to have been the oldest known fabric in the Orient, where its use for cloth is prehistoric and uninterrupted to this day. It was mentioned in the Old Testament, in Greek and Roman writers; it was related with strange exaggerations by early travelers to the East as MARCO POLO and Sir JOHN MANDEVILLE, and was used for clothing as far to the West as the army of JULIUS CÆSAR.

All of the early explorers to the portions of the western hemisphere where cotton was indigenous mention this plant and its use for cloth.

It must have been well known to the Crusaders who brought most of the luxuries to England and northern Europe. It must have been within the academic knowledge of the clergy and scholars of the laity in England, yet there did not appear to be any general use or even knowledge of cotton cloth in England until long after continental Europe and New England.

The earliest reference to cotton in an English book as far as I have been able to learn, is in " Nova Britannica ; Offering Most Excellent Fruits of Planting in Virginia," London, 1609, in which the statement is made that cotton would grow as well in that province as in Italy.

" A Declaration of the State of Virginia," London, 1620, mentions cotton among the " naturall commodities dispersed up and downe the divers parts of the world all of which may be had in abundance in Virginia."

It should be noted that these citations refer to prospective cultivation of cotton, rather than to it as a commercial commodity, and passing by certain references in letters, the earliest mention in an English book of cotton as merchandise to be received in England is said to be " Treasure of Traffic," by LEWIS ROBERTS, 1641, in which it is related that cotton woole had been received in London from islands in the Mediterranean and thence sent to Manchester. Later records show that it was used for beds, and I have been unable to find any reference precisely indicating when cotton spinning and weaving was begun in England.

Barbadoes and other of the West Indies were settled by the English at about the same time as Massachusetts Bay, and cotton from these islands was sent to England as well as to American colonists. Obstructive navigation laws were a hindrance to its importation, and the spinning of this fibre in the old country must have been conducted from the first on a very limited scale, and evidently without that commercial importance, which was the case in New England.

The Poor Law of ELIZABETH, 1601, cites the raw materials used in manufacture, and yet makes no reference to cotton, as would have been the case if it was spun at that day.

SAMUEL PEPYS records in his diary, February 27, 1663-64,

"Great good company at dinner, among others Sir MARTIN NOELL, who told us the dispute between him as farmer of the Additional Duty, and the East India Company, whether callicos be linnen or no, which he says it is, having ever been esteemed so; they say it is made of cotton woole which grows upon trees and not like flax or hemp. But it was carried against the company, though they stand out against the verdict."

Would that we knew the results of the appeal against the intrepidity of ignorance in this departmental ruling, but the gossipy diarist does not make any later record on the subject, and as he would have gloated over the' discomfiture of the reversal of the ruling, it is assumed that the Calicut cloth was legally adjudged to be "some sort of linnen."

Yet the Colony of Massachusetts Bay was legislating upon "cotton woole" as a well-known commercial raw material twenty-four years before this time.

Two notes of record on the early use of cotton in this country may be revelant in this connection.

CHRISTOPHER COLUMBUS, who was the son of a weaver, discovered in this hemisphere, corn, cotton and tobacco, but does not appear to have regarded them as anything out of the ordinary of expected curiosities, so great was his eagerness for gold and gems. In his diary he relates that after he had left the Island of San Salvador on the occasion of his first landing, the natives swam out to the boats, bearing balls of cotton thread as presents, and later in the evening came out to the ships in their canoes, with more balls of cotton, some weighing over twenty-five pounds.

A few days later, he refers to cotton cloth used by the natives of another island, and similar references are repeated in the accounts of visiting numerous islands.

What is evidently the earliest record of cotton in this vicinity is contained in the account of CHAMPLAIN of his battle on the west shore of Lake Champlain, July 2, 1609, where he refers to arrow-proof armor worn by the chiefs, consisting of strips of hard wood bound together by cotton yarn.

This cotton could not have been raised in that vicinity, but the commerce among the Indians was exclusively barter and extended over long distances.

The Indians in the natural cotton belt in Georgia and the Carolinas are known to have spun cotton, and although any known samples of that product in the North have long gone out of existence, yet if any exclusive product of the Indians at the North has been found in the South, it is fair to assume that cotton yarn was among the articles exchanged in the barter.

The arrow heads made of the peculiar rock of Mount Kineo, at Moosehead Lake, Me., and not existing elsewhere in this country, have been found in Alabama, Ohio, and Indiana, thus showing the extent of their distribution.

The only original fabric of the Indians in Massachusetts which has been found is the plaited rather than woven cloth made of the wild hemp.

NEW ENGLAND TRADERS BEFORE THE SETTLEMENT.

When the first settlers came to Massachusetts, the Indians had to a slight extent, a red cloth made of a mixture of wool and flax, known as Shag, and probably as irritating as the shirt of NESSUS, which they had obtained from the early explorers and fishermen who had sailed along the coast for nearly twenty years, and they were eager to barter skins for cloth, which formed the basis of the trade in beaver skins and forming an important commerce for more than a generation.

The extent of these antecolonial visitations of fishermen and adventurers, along the New England coast — all of them traders,— is indicated by the "Welcome Englishmen!" of Samoset to the Plymouth Colonists, and the evident ease of communication with the Indians at all the later settlements, shows that it had been sufficient for the savages to learn considerable of the English language.

As an instance of the measure of communication and its inevitable errors at earlier dates, it will be noted that the charter of the Massachusetts Bay Colony vested to it from three miles north of the Merrimack to three miles south of the Charles, and from the Atlantic Ocean to the " South Sea" which was supposed at the time to be a branch of the ocean reaching from the west to the vicinity of the present site of Albany, N. Y.

The source of this authority was from the information received from the Indians by the earlier travellers, and probably resulted from an attempt of the Indians to communicate some information in regard to Lake Champlain, the largest body of fresh water lying within the United States.

ENGLISH RESTRICTIONS UPON COMMERCE IN CLOTH.

Commerce with the Mother Country would have been beset with difficulties even under the most adventitious conditions. Vessels were small, rarely over 100 tons even after the Revolution, and generally less than half that tonnage, and could make but two round voyages to England in a year. Freights were £3 to £4 a ton, an enormous amount in those days, which has been estimated as the equivalent of eight times that amount at the present day. Thus without considering the obstructing legislation of the Navigation Acts of England, there were legitimate commercial difficulties in the way of obtaining a supply of clothing from England, and the serious condition of affairs and the remedies which were initiated were fully set forth in the acts of that very paternal government, constituting the court of the governor and deputies which legislated upon every conceivable detail of person and property.

The English Navigation Acts, 1662-1685, intended to secure to English shipping all available commerce, among them being cotton, wool, and indigo. These acts were so contrary to the natural courses of trade that they were evaded and scarcely enforced.

The export of sheep, wool, and woolen yarns from England to the Colony was prohibited in 1665, and an export duty levied on woolen cloth, and commerce between the American colonies had been forbidden at an earlier day. These unwarrantable interferences virtually made smuggling very general among the Colonists, if such a term be fairly applicable to illegal commerce under such conditions.

The extent to which this repressive legislation failed of its purpose is shown by the fact that the Complete Tradesman issued in England in 1663 makes no mention of commerce with New England as a field of export for English woolens.

It is only fair to call attention to the skill of the Florentine merchants who bought the rough woolen cloth woven in England and dyed and finished it in a superior manner by the skill of their guilds, and not merely interfered with the English market on the continent, but also sold large quantities of it at a greatly augmented price in England.

The relations of CROMWELL with the Colony of Massachusetts Bay were fickle, although posing as a friend, restrictive legislation was enacted during the protectorate. At one time he contemplated joining the colony as its ruler, at another moving it to Jamaica, and later to transfer it to Ireland, but the roots had grown too deep.

The relations of the colony with the Mother County were summed up years later by DAVID HARTLEY, who was the sole commissioner on the part of Great Britain to sign the Treaty of Utrecht which closed the Revolution, when he declared in the House of Commons that for 150 years England had given no aid or encouragement to those who sought to establish the English race on these shores, but left them to battle with the Indians and to defend their own frontier, and forced the Colonists to buy in her market and to pay the prices which were demanded.

The Colonists realized this, and their first seal bore the Macedonian cry, " Come over and help us ! "

All parties in England appeared to be a unit in seeking to keep the Colony in an absolutely dependent commercial condition, and to permit only agriculture, lumbering, fishing and peltry.

Lord CHATHAM, the proverbial friend of the Colonies, stated

that if he had his way they would not be permitted to make a horseshoe nail.

Years later when FRANKLIN as the agent of the Colonies was asked by the Council in London, "Suppose the external duties were to be laid on the necessaries of life?" gave the amazing answer, "I do not know a single article imported into the Northern Colonies but what they can either do without or make themselves. The people will spin and work for themselves in their own houses."

Severe as this legislation may appear, it was not vindictive, but merely a correspondence course in stupidity. England was poor and needed money, therefore she taxed everything available; the people were poor and it was assumed that it would help matters if such taxation was so framed as to drive colonial customers to merchants in the Mother Country.

History repeated itself when GEORGE III. wanted the town residence of the Duke of BUCKINGHAM, and the Council stated that the Exchequer had no money. "Tax the American Colonies!" said the King. Buckingham Palace was secured, the tax levied, the minority in the Colonies ruled and the cord snapped.

INSTRUCTION IN SPINNING.

Spinning and weaving were entirely domestic occupations, until about the time of the Revolution, and there must have been considerable manufacture of cloth during the earlier days of the Colony among those who came across the Atlantic, but the younger generation were not under the instructing influence derived from the spinners from the Netherlands, and with the distracting conditions of the new country they were not continuing with the same skill, and heroic measures by the Colonists were necessary in self-defense to make provision for clothing.

Let the acts in their sequence tell the story which abounds in detail if not perspective. On November 8, 1633, the scarcity of cloth had evidently begun to conform to the commercial conditions of higher prices, as the court on that day regulated the prices of many articles adding with covert threat,

" And for lynnen & other comodities wch in regard of their close stouage & small hazard may be afforded att a cheap rate wee do advise all men to be a rule to themselues in keepeing a good conscience assureing them that if any man shall exceede the bounds of moderacon wee shall punish them seuerely."

Without citing more than typical acts of legislation, the first measure which attempted to provide a physical remedy other than attempts at commercial regulation of prices which were probably as unfeasible in the face of commercial conditions then as they have been ever since that time, was the act of May 13, 1640, which introduces provisions for industrial statistics and industrial education, and indicates that somebody had been thinking wisely and concluded that the time for action had arrived.

" This Court takeing into serios consideration the absolute necessity for the raising of the manufacture of linnen cloth, &c., doth declare that it is the intent of this Court that there shalbee an order setled about it, & therefore doth require the magistrats & deputies of the severall townes to acquaint the townesmen therewth, & to make inquiry what seede is in every towne, what men & weomen are skilfull in the braking, spining, weaving, what meanes for the pviding of wheeles & to consider wth those skilfull in that manifacture what course may bee taken to raise the materials & pduce the manifacture & what course may bee taken for teaching the boyes & girles in all townes the spining of the yarne & to returne to the next Court their severall & ioynt advise about this thing. The like consideration would bee had for the spining & weaveing of cotton woole."

This was followed by the act of October 7, 1640, giving a bounty of 25 per cent. for textile manufactures.

" For incuragment of the manifacture of linnen, woollen and cotton clothe, it is ordered that whosoever shall make any sort of the said cloathes fit for use and shall shewe the same to the next magistrat or to 2 of the deputies of this Court, upon certificate thereof to this Court or the Court of Assistants, the party shall have alowance of 3d in the shilling of the worth of such cloth according to the valewation wch shal bee certified wth it. And the said magistrate or deputies shall set such marke upon the same cloth as it may bee found to have bene alowed for ; pvided this order shall extend onely to such cloth as shalbee made wthin this iurisdiction, & the yarne heare spun also, & of such materials as shalbee raised also wthin the same, or else of cotton. This order to continue for 3 yeares next followinge."

This was evidently not entirely satisfactory, as it was repealed June 2, 1641, eight months later, and on the same date, legislation was passed indicating twice that the supply of cotton was insufficient for the existing demand, and also refering to the wild hemp which was evidently derived from the practices of the Indians with this as their only indigenous source of textiles to which reference has already been made.

" This Cort takeing into consideration the want of cloathing wch is like to come upon us the next winter & not finding any way to supply us so well as by cotton wch wee find not like to bee pvided in dew time for the present want & venderstanding withall from the certain knowledge of divrse of the court that there is a kind of wild hempe groweing plentifully all over the countrey wch if it were gathered and improved, might serve for psent supply until cotton may bee had, it is therefore ordered : "

And here follows provisions for the gathering and use of wild hemp, and its spinning mornings and evenings through the seasons " that the honest and profitable custom of England may be continued." The latter appears to be the earliest reference to spinning in the old country.

The same line of constructive legislation continues, for on June 14, 1642, the following act was passed :—

" This Cort taking into consideration the great neglect of many parents and masters in training up the children in learning & labor & other imployments wch may bee profitable to the common wealth do hereupon order & decree that in every towne the chosen men for managing the prudenciall affaires of the same shall hencefourth stand charged wth the care of the redresse of this evill. They are to take care that such as are set to keep cattle bee set to some other impliment withall as spinning upon the rock, knitting, weveing tape, & for their better pformance of this trust committed to them they may divide the towne amongst them, appointing to every of the said townsmen a certeine number of families to have speciall oersight of, they are also to pvide that a sufficient quantity of materialls as hempe, flaxe, &c., may bee raised in their severall townes & tooles and implements pvided for working out the same & for their assistance in this so needfull & beneficiall impliment, if they meete with any difficulty or opposition wch they cannot well master by their owne power, they may have recorse to some of the magistrates."

This "spinning upon the rock" is a unique reference not known to occur contemporaneously elsewhere, relative to a method of spinning obtained from the Indians. The rock was a whorl of stone or dried clay in the form of a torus, or a round doughnut in which the hole was small enough to prevent from passing through the large end of the wood spindle forming the distaff and in this manner acts as a small fly-wheel on the spindle and also keeps it in a vertical position. The clay and pottery whorls found among the Indian relics in the south-west are generally covered with elaborate decorations.

On May 14, 1656, the Court enacted further legislation whose preamble indicated an alarming state of affairs on the scarcity of cloth, which urgently called for immediate action as set forth in the act, which was in part: —

"This Cort taking into serjous consideration the present streights & necessitjes that lye vppon the countrje in respect of cloathing, which is not liked to be so plentifully suppljed from forraigne parts as in tjmes past, & not knowing any better way & meanes conduceable to our subsistence then improoving as many hands as may be in spinning woole, cotton, flaxe &c,—

"Itt is therefore ordered by this Court and the authoritje thereof, that all hands not necessarily implojde on other occasions as woemen, girles & boyes, shall and heereby are enjoyned to spinn according to theire skills & abillitje; & that the selectmen in euery toune doe consider the condicon & capacitje of euery family and, accordingly assess them at one or more spinners; & since severall familyes are necessarily imployd the greatest part of theire tjme in other buisness, yet if opportunitjes were attended, sometjme might be spared at advantage by some of them for this worke. The sajd select men shall therefore assess such familyes at half or a quarter of a spinner, according to their capacitjes ; secondly, that euery one thus assessed for a whole spiner doe, after this present yeare, 1656, spinn, for 30 weekes euery yeare, three pounds p weeke of lining, cotton, or woolen, & the select men shall take special care for the execution of this order and shall haue power to make such orders in theire respective tounes for the clearing of comous for keeping of sheepe. And the deputjes of the severall tounes are hereby required to impart the mind of the Cort, for the saving of ye seede both of hemp & flaxe."

The differences in the provisions for the enforcement of the acts of 1642 and 1656 reveals a change of conditions between the old country and the new.

In the first instance, it was entrusted to the masters, being master workmen of the English guilds who had come over presumably with the Salem colony fourteen years before, as there had been but little other immigration, and at the time of the second act, it was as much later, and these twenty-eight years added to the age of a master workman of mature age at the time of the settlement would bring him beyond active labor, and in the sere and yellow age, if indeed living.

As the guilds were not perpetuated in this country, it became necessary at the time of later legisiation to use the authority of officers of Colony and towns which had been established by the Court in developing the government of the Colony.

This legislation indicates the wonderful scope of initiative in the minds, as we find here provisions for the first public education, which was vocational and textile education, and also industrial statistics.

The oft quoted act establishing free public schools sustained by general taxation where our ancestors learned their letters from the horn book, and in the scarcity of paper learned to write and to cypher on birch bark, was not passed until 1647.

Would that we knew the man who framed the legislation which met the issue so decisively, in order that later generations might keep him in grateful remembrance for the action which undoubtedly preserved the Colony, and also served as a nucleus which in due time developed the textile manufacture of New England.

Such individual instruction was not accompanied by records to reveal the various steps and details of the work, but the more important matter of the result is known and that is, the people were adequately furnished with homespun cloth or there would have been further legislation, and some outcries in sermons, account books or inventories would have furnished a record.

There is however, one record which sums up the whole result of this stimulus both of textile education and the provisions for raw material and that is in the contemporaneous Johnson's Wonder Working Providence in New England in 1652, stating that the people made more than enough clothing for their own use.

Some clothing at a price did come from England as account books show, but it was evidently far less than required for supplying the needs of the people.

As woolen goods require to be fulled, the establishment of fulling mills were matters of record in the sale of land, development of water power, and permits to build, in settlements throughout the colony where there was a water supply for the purpose, and this gives records showing the weaving of wool, while the spinning and weaving of cotton being a domestic handicraft, made no comparable record.

Rowley appears to have been a textile headquarters which failed to develop into leading conditions for the textile manufacture in years later, probably from lack of water power and deep water transportation, as flax, hemp and cotton were woven there in large quantities before 1639 and this centering of the industry attracted twenty families of Yorkshire weavers to settle there in 1643.

THE SUPPLY OF COTTON FOR NEW ENGLAND.

The acts of the General Court show that " cotton woole " was well known in the Colony in 1636 and various records show that the earlier importation of cotton and indigo from Barbadoes, which appears to have been in many instances a generic name for the West Indies, was extensive; and this importation continued until the war of 1812.

The Desire of Salem, the largest ship of her day, returned to that port in 1638 with a large supply of cotton.

The Trial, 160 tons, was the first ship built in Boston and her first voyage was to St. Christophers in the West Indies for a cargo of cotton.

Salt fish, staves and Indian captives were sent to that fertile island in exchange for cotton, molasses, and "ye inspiring Barbadoes drynk" and negro slaves. I have been told by an observant traveller that Indians sent there and intermarrying with the negroes were sufficient to hybridize the kink in the wool to a wave, remaining to this day nearly three centuries in anticipation of the skill of MARCEL, the coffieur.

The state of Connecticut in 1640 imported cotton from the West Indies and sold it to their towns, and private enterprise undoubtedly obtained it at an earlier day, as in the Colony of Massachusetts Bay.

The packing of cotton gave trouble then and remains a live issue to this day, as an organization was formed in Boston last February to mitigate this difficulty.

JOHN HULL, the most enterprising Boston merchant of his day and the treasurer of the Commonwealth for many years, writes that he had received from the West Indies two bags of "vile cotton woole," which he sends to a customer who evidently comes to the same opinion when he finds in the middle of a bag "much fowle cotton" and makes reclamation upon HULL who is obliged to make amends. Evidently the "dogtail" grade has no claim as modern slang.

The supply of cotton was provided for by an active export trade in what was practically a foreign product, until long after the invention of the American cotton gin by ELI WHITNEY in 1793 which provided for the raw material the entirely different commercial conditions of cotton manufacturing.

THE SUPPLY OF WOOL.

The shortage of wool received due attention of the Court by the act of August 22, 1654, in which the growth of sheep was encouraged by an act whose preamble stated that:—

" Whereas this countrje is at this tjme in great streights in respect of cloathing, and the most likeljest way tending to our supply in that respect is the rajsing and keeping of sheepe wthin our jurisdiccon,"

and in detail the exporting of ewes is forbidden as well as the injunction that none shall be killed until they are two years old.

The effect of these and earlier provisions for increase of sheep for the sake of their wool was little short of marvellous.

There were 1,000 sheep in Massachusetts Bay Colony in 1642, and in 1660 the English Council made a report that the Colony had 100,000 sheep and was also buying wool from the Dutch. At the earlier date at least they were sending staves and salt fish to Spain which were traded for wool.

CORDAGE.

Vessels of that day were equipped with revolving hooks for laying cordage which was the first textile manufacturing of the Colony. These rope-making heads turned by hand, contined without serious modifications until recent time, about 200 years after the landing, were also set up on shore and rope making carried on at first in the open, but there was so much available space for this purpose that information on the subject comes by way of incident rather than designed record. In this way, it is known that JOHN and PHILIP VAREN made rope in Salem in 1635, and JOHN HARRISON, on Purchase street, at Boston in 1641, and there were others wherever rope was wanted and hemp available, and it was not until there was a larger population after the next century came in that there appears any legislation on the subject other than the early acts of the court relative to the cultivation and treatment of hemp already cited, and these pertained to its ultimate use for weaving.

In the later days, we learn that the selectmen of Boston on April 12, 1702, allowed EDWARD GRAY to make use of the highway near Lieutenant HOLMES to make ropes at a rent of twenty shillings a year in the future and seven shillings a year in the past, and later, on May 17, 1708, the town of Boston gave " EDWARD SHEAF leaf to set up some posts in the training field to make ropes on." After the rope walks between Pearl and Atkinson (now Congress) streets had been destroyed by fire and considered to be a hazard to the buildings in that vicinity, the town granted in 1794 lands west of Charles street and the Common which were called " rope walk lands." The ropes were first made in the open, but as this was too much of a pleasant weather business like the making of hay, four covered rope walks were built and these later proved to be such a fire hazard to buildings which had extended in that direction, at the fire which destroyed them in 1806, that after several years' negotiations the city bought the lands in 1828 for $35,000, and the tract forms the present Public Garden.

The problem in regard to cordage was that of the raw material and not its method of manufacture, as every sailor knew how to lay hemp, and there was no need of legislation upon its manufacture.

THE SPINNING SCHOOLS OF BOSTON.

About 1720 the question of instruction in spinning took a distinctively different position from that of the Colony seventy years before.

In place of a system organized on the basis of individual instruction to small groups, in the fields or elsewhere working with distaff or in a dwelling at a spinning wheel, there was a general movement for vocational schools, although they left that word and not much else as to methods for modern instructors.

The suddenness of the achievement and its grasp upon the community was remarkable, and while there must have been some cause for a sentiment which enlisted the intense affiliation of all classes of the community, yet the economic principle which must have existed does not appear in any marked change of commercial or sociological conditions.

Although there are no citations to confirm the opinion, yet it appears as if this movement must have had some connection with the organized opposition of the English spinners and weavers of cotton, which found voice in the English law of 1721 forbidding the wearing of dyed or printed cotton goods " except blue calicoes, muslins or fustians." The first two of which at that time were imported from Calcutta, and indicated the hand of the powerful East India Company in amending legislation.

The people of New England had grown to appreciate cotton, which was then as it is now the cheapest of fibres, and naturally desired to provide for its continuance before any similar prohibitions should be attempted for New England by the mother country.

While allusion is made to the poor in some of the records, they were " always with us," and as the spinning schools were begun seventy years after the establishment of public schools, there is nothing in any such references to warrant an opinion that they were tributary to a mendicant class, but it is evident that they were framed for the general welfare of the community.

It is unfair for some writers to apply the term " spinning craze" to this movement, as instead of being ephemeral, it endured for over fifty years, when it was stopped by the stirring events of the Revolution.

The endorsement of these schools by those of social position was indicated by the establishment of organizations of ladies who would meet and spin, while the clergyman would discourse to them, and the easy running Saxony wheel did not disturb the spinning of yarns while that of yarn went on.

Shortly before the Revolution, these spinning societies took an important part in stirring up local zeal, as serving a similar purpose to what has been done by other organizations equally far afield from their original object in movements preceding political overturns in many countries.

The reiteration of considering, referring to committees,

resolving, and appropriating for spinning schools, drags its weary way through fifty and more years of town records.

The records for the most part fail to indicate what was actually accomplished, but the fact of the renewal of the resolutions on the subject indicates that the former measures had not been permanent, but that the purpose of the people was unchanged.

In the perspective of nearly two centuries, the years appear close together, and the brief records omit the obvious of that day, but the very pertinacy with which the subject was attacked by so many different people with their varied points of view during two generations, indicate these measures appealed to public sentiment as a living need.

Without assuming to cite in detail, a general review of this industrial movement will illustrate the definite purpose of a community for over half a century.

Long preliminary to the establishment of these schools, the selectmen of Boston on April 13, 1702, voted to buy some spinning wheels to provide work for the poor, evidently an instance of that wisest form of charity which places the needy in a self-supporting condition.

It should be noted that in 1718, a number of Irish spinners arrived and were assigned land on the west side of the Merrimac river below Manchester, N. H. The site was unsatisfactory and many of them moved to different parts of the Province, especially to Boston, where they excited the enthusiasm of the people for spinning, and a spinning school was formed by them which met on the Common before the establishment of spinning schools by the town. It may be worth the while to note that these people introduced the cultivation of the first potatoes into New England, although they had been brought in small quantities from Bermuda as early as 1636, and were served as a rarity at Harvard College commencement dinner in 1708.

The town of Boston voted on March 14, 1720, to establish a spinning school in which the pupils had not merely free instruction but board for the first three months and after that time the yarn should be bought from them, and also premiums for good work. Three hundred pounds were loaned to the school for seven years, and twenty spinning wheels ordered.

DANIEL OLIVER, a Boston merchant, one of the Royal Council, and also chairman of the town committee appointed to establish a spinning school in 1720, built at an expense of £600 a spinning school next to Barton's Ropewalk near to the Craigie Bridge, for the use of the town, to which he bequeathed the building. He died July 23, 1731. This appears to be the site of the spinning school, although the report of the committee at the meeting December 27, 1720, recommended as the site of the spinning school, the " cellar most made " in front of Captain SOUTHACKS, which is the site of the Scollay building formerly in Scollay's square but I do not find any record of the acquisition of the site or the construction of the building, although several histories refer to Scollay's Square as the site of the school.

This subject was further taken up by a town meeting September 28, 1720, which according to some authorities, resulted in the erection of a large building known as the Manufactory House on Long Acre (now Tremont) Street, where Hamilton Place now enters. A large figure of a woman with a distaff was painted on the westerly wall.

Although both the records and local histories contain many references to this building which was an important feature in industrial development, but little is known about it. It is quite probable that the name was applied to two buildings, or to extensive enlargements of the first one, as there is evidence of purchase of land and expenditures on the building by the Province on the Manufactory House up to the summer of 1754.

The reference to the provision of board for the pupils was so inconsistent with a town school, as to raise a query which was answered in part by the action of the Provincial Legislature purchasing the Manufactory House in 1748, and granted to the town of Boston four townships for its support and the use of the Provincial Frigate for the transportation of the scholars.

In 1735 the Province levied a tax on carriages to support the spinning school and this statute was repealed in 1753, in which year the town of Boston passed an ordinance for a similar tax for the same purpose.

This provincial legislation on the school and its maintenance indicates that it was a provincial as well as a town institution, and gives a reason why board was provided for the scholars.

In 1762 the Manufactory House was ordered sold, but the sale did not take place, perhaps from lack of a purchaser, and it remained standing until 1806, when Hamilton Place was run through its site.

When this spinning school was opened there was a large spinning bee on the common where many women operated their spinning wheels. Chief Justice SAMUEL SEWALL, who was the moderator of the town meeting when the spinning school was authorized, presided on this occasion.

In 1753, on the fourth anniversary of the society, there was another large spinning bee held on the common at which 300 weavers were in three rows, with their leader borne on the shoulders of men, and a large number of weavers with their leader weaving on a raised platform. Rev. Dr. SAMUEL COOPER "improved" the occasion by a discourse. This affair attracted to the town the largest number of people ever known at any one time.

The town of Boston voted in 1754 to use the Old Town House on the site of the present Old State House, for a spinning school and appropriated £50, old tenor, to put the building in repair.

Charlestown had taken similar action in regard to its old town house the preceding year.

Another movement in textile instruction is indicated by the town notice September 2, 1762, that the spinning school in the Manufactory House is again opened and that any person may learn to spin without charge and be paid for their spinning after the first three months, and that a premium of £18 old tenor is offered to the four best spinners.

At a town meeting April 4, 1769, a committee of which WILLIAM MOLYNEAUX, a leading Boston merchant of Huguenot ancestry, born in 1716 and died October 22, 1774, was the chairman, reported in favor of setting up spinning schools in various parts of the city, and hiring rooms and spinning wheels, and the employment of school mistresses, and buying wool which "can be converted into shalloons, durants, pamblitts, callamancoes, durois, legathies, and in general men's summer wear." None of these fabrics are known by this name today, or indeed what manner of cloth, other than they were woolen goods.

The action of the town varied somewhat from the recommendation of the committee. The whole project was put into the hands of Mr. MOLYNEAUX to whom the town gave £200 to purchase equipment and hire rooms and employ school mistresses, and also loaned him £300 to purchase wool.

I have been unable to learn anything of the several places which it was authorized should be hired for this purpose, except that the Manufactory House was granted him for the purpose for seven years at an annual rental of five peppercorns. It should be remembered that this building was then the property of the Province and not of the town.

A year later, March, 1770, we learn that he had a large number of spinning wheels and had engaged rooms for enabling many young women to earn their support.

The energy of Mr. MOLYNEAUX inspired great activity in spinning schools throughout the community outside of Boston and large quantities of cotton and woolen goods were made.

In this good work Mr. MOLYNEAUX had personally advanced amounts beyond the appropriations, and at the town meeting in March, 1770, he requested a further allowance from the town in reimbursement, but the question was laid over until an adjourned meeting when Justice DANA could be present and give legal advice and at the later meeting Justice DANA was in attendance and gave his opinion that he doubted whether the town could legally remit the amount asked for, and no further action was taken except to give Mr. MOLYNEAUX, "a vote of thanks for his faithful discharge relative to the spinning business."

While Mr. MOLYNEAUX may have longed for an hour of Judge SEWELL, who presided at the town meeting when spinning schools were authorized fifty years before, he did not rest here, but at once presented a memorial to the General Court in which for the first time during this fifty years there is any disclosure of methods and equipment of this succession of spinning schools, and this action also indicates the close relation between town and Province in regard to these schools.

He states that they have thoroughly instructed at least three hundred children in the art of spinning, and to whom a large amount has been later paid in wages, and that he has received only a loan from the town of £500 without interest, while between £11,000 and £12,000 has been expended in fitting up the machinery; the first amount is evidently old tenor, but not the later ones.

The equipment of this institution is interesting as it includes on hand 40,000 skeins of fine yarn fit to make any kind of women's wear and a large amount of dyestuffs; and for the plant, a large number of spinning wheels which he had made, also "complete apparatus" among which is cited twisting and winding mills, fifty looms, furnaces for hot and cold presses, and dyehouse with large copper tanks.

There does not appear to be any record showing that this memorial received different treatment from the usual government claim, but whatever may have been the injustice of town and Province, the official record shows that the people owed a great debt of gratitude to this wise merchant in giving of his skill and his fortune toward the extension of the textile art in such a manner that the immediate results made many women self-supporting at a time when the opportunities for work outside of domestic employment were few.

I have omitted all reference to the long continued petitions, votes and appropriations relative to the linen duck manufacture in the town of Boston, as it was at best a manufacturing scheme, or a succession of them, by promoters which was brought to an end by the granting of a petition to discharge the obligations of the surviving members of the Linen Manufactory as the enterprise had been a failure. It does not appear that there ever was any provision for the textile education of the young in the enterprise.

Sails in northern countries were always made of linen, until SETH BEMIS made duck from sea island cotton at Watertown in 1809. A few years ago sea island cotton was used in making at New Hartford, Conn., a set of sails for one of the defenders of the International cup.

In closing this account of the sagacity and enterprise in textiles of the people of Massachusetts Bay, it may be well to note that an important provision for the beginnings of the manufacture of cotton goods at about the time of the Revolution rested upon the wisdom of Governor JOHN WINTHROP, who in 1633 encouraged the development of all water powers near to settlements for grain mills and saw mills.

These mills are said to have been generally built of stone and were one story in height. One hundred and fifty years later when power spinning machinery was surreptitiously imported, many of these grain and saw mills were extended a story higher with wood, and there were twenty-seven such spinning mills in Massachusetts before 1812, — none of which are believed to be now standing,— but the charter and vested rights of many a water-power in this Commonwealth rest upon the run-of-stone which they must still retain.

The inventions of the spinning jenney by HARGREAVES in 1667, and the spinning frame by ARKWRIGHT in 1769, which surreptitiously reached this country just before the Revolution were the beginning of the end of making cloth solely as a domestic occupation, and cotton manufacturing had begun.

It should be stated there was always one marked difference between hand made cotton goods in Old England and New England, that whereas in New England such cloth was made entirely of cotton, and inventories in Colonial times show that it was appraised at a higher price than linen, but pure hand-made cotton was not made in Old England until after 1760, but was woven with linen warp and cotton filling, yet the English imported a large amount of calico, which was the trade name for cotton cloth obtained from Calcutta whether white ·or hand printed.

The extent of cotton manufacture involves amounts " beyond the dreams of avarice," and yet its increase had been largely the additional use by those within the zone of the cotton manufacture. Civilized people are using an increased amount of cotton cloth both in elaboration of dress, and of late years in the substitution of cotton for wool, either pure or mixed in many fabrics.

Yet the cotton manufacture has hardly made its mark among the unnumbered millions of the Orient or the barbarous people of warm countries. It has been estimated that only about 20 to 25 per cent. of the population of the earth wearing cotton cloth,· use manufactured goods.

Labor in those countries is so cheap and land transportation so dear, that the differences in cost generally equate themselves in a distance of fifty miles from navigable waters.

The great amount of concentration of human skill in the cotton manufacture has accomplished wonderful results in reducing the cost of the manufactured product, and therefore extending its usage.

Although it may have made the cheaper class of goods more uniform in their quality, yet the finer varieties of fabrics still continue to be the result of handicraft.

The finest muslins are still spun and woven by hand in India by a cult whose skill was well established at the time of the earliest acquisitions of authority by the East India Company in that country.

The artistic weaving of the World is that of the Gobelins, who still maintain handicraft methods at their little Flemish Colony in Paris, where they were established by Louis XIV., who ·also introduced the Merino sheep into France.